Chapters:

While "A breath of fresh air" isn't strictly aviation slang, it is commonly used within the aviation community with specific nuances. Here's a breakdown:

Definition:

•Original: Something new, positive, and invigorating that brings a welcome change from monotony or negativity.

•Aviation context: Can refer to:

•A new, innovative aircraft design or technology.

•A young, skilled pilot demonstrating promising abilities.

•A clear day with excellent visibility after days of bad weather.

•A humorous or insightful message over the radio that breaks the routine.

Modern translation:

•Something refreshing, exciting, or uplifting.

•A welcome change of pace or perspective.

Origin:

•The phrase itself predates aviation and is found in general English as early as the 17th century.

•Its adoption in aviation likely stems from the inherent desire for novelty and positive experiences within the demanding and routine environment of flying.

Sentence example:

•Pilot 1: "Man, flying the same routes day after day gets old. Today's student pilot, though, she's a real breath of fresh air. Sharp as a tack and keeps things interesting."

•Tower: "Attention all aircraft, visibility just improved significantly. Feels like a breath of fresh air up here after that storm! Enjoy the clear skies."

Additional notes:

•While not exclusive to aviation, the specific application of "breath of fresh air" within the context reflects the unique culture and challenges of the flying environment.

•The term can also be used sarcastically, depending on the tone and delivery.

In the context of aviation, "airs and graces" doesn't have a specific slang meaning. It holds its original, more general meaning:

Definition:

•Original: Behaving in a way that shows you think you are more important than other people, in a snobbish or arrogant manner.

•Aviation context: Not typically used in this literal sense for pilots or aircraft.

•Possible figurative use: Could metaphorically describe an aircraft performing exceptionally smooth and graceful maneuvers, like a show plane showcasing its capabilities. However, this usage is not common and would depend heavily on the specific context.

Origin:

•The phrase "airs and graces" dates back to the 16th century in English and originally referred to elegant or affected manners.

Modern translation:

•Snobbish, arrogant, or condescending behavior.

•(Figuratively, rarely used in aviation) Exceptionally smooth and elegant flying.

Sentence example (original meaning):

•While most pilots are down-to-earth and professional, I've encountered a few with real "airs and graces," looking down on those with less experience.

Sentence example (figurative meaning, uncommon):

•The experimental aircraft danced through the air with incredible grace, truly displaying its "airs and graces" during the airshow.

Important note: Using "airs and graces" in a figurative sense within aviation is very uncommon and could be misinterpreted. It's generally safer to stick to the original meaning unless you're confident your audience will understand your specific, intended usage.

While "ahead of the curve" isn't exclusive to aviation slang, it has interesting usage and possible origin within the field:

Definition:

•General: Being aware of and prepared for future trends or changes before they become mainstream.

•Aviation context:

•Can refer to:

•Pilots who adopt new technologies or flying techniques early on.

•Airlines implementing innovative strategies to stay competitive.

•Aircraft manufacturers designing next-generation models with advanced features.

•Often associated with safety advancements, efficiency improvements, and environmental consciousness.

Modern translation:

•Proactive, innovative, and forward-thinking.

•Anticipating and adapting to change effectively.

Origin:

•The phrase itself predates aviation and possibly originated in mathematics or economics, referencing staying ahead of trends represented as curves on a graph.

•Its adoption in aviation likely stems from the constant need for innovation and adaptation in a rapidly evolving field.

Sentence example:

•"This young pilot is truly ahead of the curve. She's already mastered drone piloting and is actively involved in researching sustainable aviation fuels."

•"The airline's decision to invest in electric planes shows they're truly ahead of the curve in embracing environmentally friendly technologies."

Additional notes:

•"Ahead of the curve" can sometimes carry a connotation of being ahead of the pack or even elitist, depending on the context and delivery.

In aviation, "by the seat of your pants" is a well-known idiom, but it doesn't literally mean that pilots control the aircraft based on how they feel in their pants! Here's the breakdown:

Definition:

•Original: Making decisions and taking action based on instinct, experience, and immediate reactions, rather than on extensive planning or specific instructions.

•Aviation context: This used to be more relevant in the early days of flight, when instruments were limited, and pilots relied heavily on their senses and intuition to navigate.

•Modern aviation: While still occasionally used figuratively, it generally denotes improvising or adapting in unexpected situations, even with the aid of modern technology. It can be seen as a negative if it implies a lack of preparation or disregard for procedures, but also positive if it highlights resourceful piloting in emergencies.

Modern translation:

•Improvising, winging it, making it up as you go.

•Reacting to situations without a predefined plan.

•(Sometimes) Flying without strict adherence to procedures.

Origin:

•The exact origin is unclear, but theories suggest it could relate to:

•Early pilots feeling aircraft movements through their seats without instruments.

•The quick reactions and improvisation needed in early, less-controlled flights.

Sentence example

•"With engine failure looming, the experienced pilot had to fly by the seat of her pants and managed a safe emergency landing."

Important notes:

•The interpretation of "flying by the seat of your pants" in aviation depends on the context and tone.

•It's generally used figuratively in modern times, with actual flights relying heavily on instruments and procedures.

•While sometimes implying improvisation, it doesn't always carry a negative connotation, depending on the pilot's skill and the situation.

While "bought the farm" is commonly used in general slang to mean "passed away," it's not typically used in aviation with that specific meaning. It has different origins and applications within the aviation world:

Possible Origins in Aviation:

1.Crash Landing: Some theories suggest it originated from World War II pilots expressing a desire to stop flying and buy a farm after the war. If they died in service, it was said they "bought the farm" metaphorically, referring to their unfulfilled wish. However, this lacks concrete evidence.

2.Damaged Land: Another theory proposes it arose from wartime situations where farmers whose land was damaged by military aircraft crashes received compensation, essentially "buying the farm" with the insurance money. This theory also lacks strong historical support.

Current Usage in Aviation:

1.Informal Jargon: "Bought the farm" is rarely used literally in today's aviation, especially due to its potentially insensitive implications. Some older pilots or mechanics might occasionally use it humorously or metaphorically, but it's not widespread or universally understood.

2.Humorous Misinterpretations: Due to its general meaning of death, non-aviation individuals might misinterpret its use within aviation, possibly causing offense or misunderstanding. It's generally best to avoid using it altogether in aviation communication.

Alternatives:

If referring to a fatal accident, respectful and professional terms like "aircraft accident," "tragic loss," or "passed away" are recommended. Humor or slang involving death is best avoided in most aviation contexts.

In aviation, "cleared to approach" is not considered slang, but rather a critical and well-defined communication phrase between Air Traffic Control (ATC) and pilots. Here's the breakdown:

Definition:

•Official meaning: ATC authorization for an aircraft to execute a specific instrument approach procedure to an airport. It means the pilot is cleared to descend and follow a published path towards landing.

•Additional details:

•The "approach" in the phrase specifies the type of procedure (e.g., ILS, GPS, VOR) and runway.

•"Cleared to approach" doesn't guarantee immediate landing clearance. Sequencing and other factors often apply.

•Pilots acknowledge the clearance with a response like "cleared to approach runway XX, [aircraft callsign]."

Modern translation:

•Permission to begin the final descent for landing, following a specific path.

•Not the same as landing clearance, which comes later in the landing sequence.

Origin:

•This phrase predates aviation slang and stems from standard aviation communication protocols established to ensure safety and clarity.

Sentence example:

•"Tower, Cessna 1234 is requesting a vector for the ILS approach to runway 18."

•"Cessna 1234, cleared for the ILS approach to runway 18, maintain 3000 feet until established on the localizer."

•"Cessna 1234, cleared to approach runway 18, maintain 3000 feet until established on the localizer."

Important notes:

•"Cleared to approach" is a vital part of safe and efficient landing procedures.

•Understanding this phrase and related aviation terminology is crucial for pilots and anyone interested in learning about aviation communication.

In aviation, "crash and burn" isn't typically used literally, unlike its general slang meaning of failing spectacularly. However, it has some interesting nuances within the aviation world:

Original Meaning:

•Literal: Refers to an aircraft physically crashing and catching fire, resulting in destruction and potential loss of life.

Figurative Usage in Aviation:

1.Informal Jargon: While uncommon, some may use it metaphorically to describe:

•A poorly executed landing with a rough touchdown.

•A risky maneuver that almost ends in disaster.

•A failed flight attempt due to technical issues.

•A pilot's career ending abruptly due to mistakes or incidents.

2.Historical Reference: The term might echo the very real dangers of early aviation, where crashes and fires were unfortunately more common.

Current Relevance:

•Modern aviation: With safety advancements and strict regulations, literal "crash and burn" scenarios are thankfully rare.

•Sensitivity: Due to its potential association with real-life tragedies, using "crash and burn" lightly or humorously within aviation can be insensitive and disrespectful.

•Alternatives: More professional and respectful terms like "accident," "incident," "hard landing," "technical difficulty," or "career change" are preferred when referring to negative situations.

Remember:

•While "crash and burn" has historical roots in aviation, its literal meaning is thankfully uncommon in modern times.

•Using it figuratively is best avoided due to potential insensitivity and misinterpretations.

•Choosing respectful and professional language is crucial when discussing any incidents or challenges within aviation.

While "Fangs sunk in floorboard" isn't a common aviation idiom, it has two possible interpretations within the field:

1. Figurative Expression:

•Meaning: This interpretation depicts a pilot pushing the aircraft to its limits, experiencing intense focus and determination during a challenging maneuver. It evokes an image of gripping the controls tightly, as if digging metaphorical "fangs" into the floorboard for extra control.

•Origin: Unclear; it might be an informal invention within certain pilot communities or used in aviation-themed fictional works.

•Usage: Primarily metaphorical, describing high-performance flying or intense piloting situations.

•Example: "The test pilot pushed the experimental aircraft to its limits, fangs sunk in floorboard, as she evaluated its maneuverability."

2. Historical Reference:

•Meaning: Some speculate it might be a historical reference to early open-cockpit aircraft, where pilots literally wore leather helmets with goggles, resembling fangs, and held onto the floorboards for stability during rough flights.

•Origin: Highly theoretical; lacks concrete historical evidence.

•Usage: Very uncommon, mostly as a historical anecdote or speculation.

•Example: "In the days of barnstorming and open cockpits, pilots flew with fangs sunk in floorboard, braving the elements and pushing the boundaries of flight."

Important Notes:

•"Fangs sunk in floorboard" is not a widely recognized expression in aviation.

•Its interpretation depends on context and intended meaning.

•Using it metaphorically can be understood by some, but exercise caution due to its potentially unusual nature.

•It's crucial to prioritize respectful and clear communication in aviation settings.

"Fly by" has a few different interpretations in the context of aviation, depending on the specific situation and context:

1. Informal Communication:

•Meaning: This is a casual way for pilots to inform others about their planned route or location. It can be used in various ways:

•"Just flying by to say hello!" (Informal greeting over the radio)

•"Flying by the airport, will be landing shortly." (Announcing arrival)

•"Doing a fly-by over the city for a photo shoot." (Describing a specific maneuver)

•Origin: Informal adoption within pilot communities, similar to other casual expressions used in communication.

•Usage: Primarily in informal communication between pilots or enthusiasts.

•Example: "Tower, Cessna 1234 just flying by for a scenic tour, no landing planned."

2. Technical Maneuver:

•Meaning: In some cases, "fly-by" can refer to a specific technical maneuver, such as:

•Low-altitude fly-by: A low-altitude pass over a specific point, often used for military demonstrations or training.

•High-speed fly-by: A high-speed pass over a point, used for testing aircraft performance or creating sonic booms.

•Origin: Technical term used in aviation manuals and procedures.

•Usage: Primarily in technical contexts or discussions about specific maneuvers.

•Example: "The test pilots conducted a high-speed fly-by to collect data on the aircraft's aerodynamics."

3. Military Operations:

•Meaning: In military contexts, "fly-by" can refer to:

•Show of force: A military aircraft demonstration to display power or intimidate an adversary.

•Reconnaissance mission: A quick fly-over of an area to gather information.

•Origin: Military terminology used in operational planning and communication.

•Usage: Primarily in military contexts and discussions about specific operations.

•Example: "The fighter jets conducted a fly-by over the enemy base as a show of force."

"Fly off the handle" isn't specific to aviation slang, but it occasionally pops up in the context of pilot behavior, usually metaphorically. Here's the breakdown:

Original Meaning:

•General: To become suddenly and uncontrollably angry, lose one's temper.

•Origin: Unclear, possibly linked to an axe head flying off its handle due to loose fitting.

Aviation Context:

•Metaphorical Use: Pilots typically prioritize calm and collected decision-making. So, "flying off the handle" figuratively describes a pilot:

•Losing composure or acting impulsively in a stressful situation.

•Reacting angrily to unexpected issues or ATC instructions.

•Demonstrating unprofessional behavior during communication or interactions.

•Usage: Not common, generally avoided in professional settings due to negative connotations.

•Example (Negative): "The pilot reportedly 'flew off the handle' during a turbulence encounter, yelling at ATC and jeopardizing the safety of the flight."

Important Notes:

•Using "fly off the handle" in aviation, even metaphorically, can be risky due to its potential misinterpretation and negative implications.

•It's crucial for pilots to maintain professionalism and composure in all situations.

•Alternative, more descriptive terms like "lost composure," "acted impulsively," or "demonstrated unprofessional behavior" are preferred for clear and factual communication.

"Fly under the radar" is another great one, and it certainly holds meaning in the aviation world, both literally and figuratively.

Literal Meaning:
•In its most basic sense, "flying under the radar" refers to an aircraft flying at an altitude that isn't detected by radar systems. This could be done for various reasons, including:
•Military operations: Evading enemy detection during wartime or covert missions.
•Smuggling: Avoiding authorities tracking illegal activities.
•Low-altitude sightseeing: Enjoying scenic views while staying below radar coverage.
However, it's important to note that intentionally flying under the radar without proper authorization is highly dangerous and illegal, posing significant safety risks and potential legal consequences.

Figurative Meaning:
More commonly in aviation and general speech, "flying under the radar" takes on a metaphorical meaning:
•To avoid attracting attention, operate discreetly, or stay unnoticed.
•To go about something quietly, without making a big fuss or announcement.
•To operate outside the mainstream or established norms.
This figurative usage can apply to pilots who prefer quiet routes, airlines with unique strategies, or even new aircraft designs undergoing testing before public release.

Origin:
The idiom's origin likely stems from military contexts, where pilots strategically flew below radar detection to avoid being targeted. Over time, it transcended the literal aviation sense and entered general language to describe any situation where someone or something operates discreetly.

Examples:
•Literal: "The experimental aircraft flew under the radar to gather data without attracting attention."
•Figurative: "The young pilot preferred to fly under the radar, taking scenic routes and avoiding busy airspace."
•Figurative: "The airline launched its new service quietly, flying under the radar of its competitors."

"Flying by the seat of your pants" is a classic aviation idiom, but its meaning and usage have evolved over time. Let's delve into its nuances:

Original Meaning:

•Literal: Early pilots, lacking sophisticated instruments, relied heavily on their physical sensations to control aircraft. "Flying by the seat of your pants" could literally describe feeling the aircraft's movements through the seat.

Modern Meaning:

•Figurative: Today, it signifies making decisions and taking action based on instinct, experience, and immediate reactions rather than extensive planning or specific instructions. While pilots still rely on instruments, this phrase highlights situations where improvisation and quick thinking are essential.

Interpretations:

•Negative: Can imply a lack of preparation or disregard for established procedures, especially in safety-critical situations.

•Positive: Can highlight resourceful piloting and adaptability in emergencies or unexpected situations.

Modern Usage:

•Less common in actual flight operations due to advanced technology and strict procedures.

•More prevalent in informal contexts or fictional portrayals of aviation.

Alternatives:

•More neutral: "Adapting to the situation," "making real-time decisions," "utilizing experience."

•More positive: "Quick thinking," "resourceful piloting," "demonstrating airmanship."

Important Notes:

•Consider the context and tone when using or interpreting "flying by the seat of your pants" in aviation settings.

•Avoid using it to describe actual flight operations to maintain professionalism and clarity.

•Choose more precise and objective language when discussing critical situations or procedures.

"Flying high" isn't strictly an aviation idiom, but it does have interesting applications within the field and beyond. Here's a breakdown:

Original Meaning:

•General: To be feeling very successful, happy, or optimistic. Often used metaphorically to describe a sense of euphoria or achievement.

Aviation Context:

•Figurative Use: Pilots and aviation enthusiasts might use it figuratively to describe:

•Personal achievements like obtaining a pilot's license, mastering a new skill, or successfully completing a challenging flight.

•The success of an airline, aviation company, or new aircraft program.

•The general feeling of freedom and exhilaration associated with flying.

Modern Usage:

•This phrase transcends aviation and is widely used in everyday language to express success, happiness, or optimism.

Origin:

•The exact origin is unclear, but its association with positive feelings likely stems from the uplifting experience of flight and the metaphorical connection to soaring high above challenges.

Examples:

•Aviation: "She's been flying high ever since she aced her pilot's license exam."

•Figurative: "The company's stock is flying high after their successful product launch."

•General: "Feeling fly high today after achieving my fitness goals."

Important Notes:

•While commonly used, "flying high" can be considered informal or slang depending on the context.

•In professional aviation settings, more specific and objective language might be preferred for clarity and accuracy.

In aviation, "follow your nose" isn't a common expression with a specific meaning like some other idioms you've mentioned. However, it could be interpreted in a few different ways depending on the context:

Informal Instruction:

•Pilots might use it playfully or humorously to tell someone to:

•Fly in a straight line or towards a visible landmark. This would be a very informal and imprecise instruction, not used in actual navigation.

•Look closely and rely on their visual observation. This could be relevant in visual identification tasks or when situational awareness is crucial.

Metaphorical Use:

•It could be used metaphorically to encourage someone to:

•Trust their instincts and intuition in an uncertain situation. This would emphasize using judgment and experience alongside available information.

•Be bold and decisive, taking initiative and following their chosen course. This wouldn't apply to situations with strict procedures or safety requirements.

Important Notes:

•"Follow your nose" is not a standard phrase used in aviation communication due to its ambiguity and potential for misinterpretation.

•In professional settings, pilots rely on accurate information and established procedures for navigation and decision-making.

•When encountering this phrase, consider the speaker's intent and ensure clear communication is maintained for safety and clarity.

Potential Alternatives:

•Precise navigation instructions: Use specific headings, waypoints, or instrument readings for clear guidance.

•Encouragement or trust: Phrase it more explicitly like "trust your judgment" or "go with your gut" for better understanding.

In aviation, "full of hot air" has two potential interpretations, depending on the context:

Literal Meaning:

•This refers to a hot air balloon, which uses heated air inside its envelope to achieve buoyancy and fly. So, saying something is "full of hot air" could directly reference this type of aircraft.

•This meaning is uncommon in most aviation conversations but might be used playfully or humorously, especially among enthusiasts or balloon pilots.

Figurative Meaning:

•This is the more common interpretation, borrowed from general language and applied metaphorically within aviation. It describes someone who:

•Talks a lot but says little of substance, boasting or exaggerating claims without much supporting evidence.

•Provides unrealistic or unfounded advice or instructions.

•Makes grand promises without the ability or intention to follow through.

Usage:

•This figurative meaning is informal and typically used in casual conversations or personal opinions. It should be avoided in professional settings due to its negative connotations and potential to insult or offend someone.

Important Notes:

•Using "full of hot air" figuratively in aviation can be risky, as interpretations may vary. It's important to consider the listener's perspective and potential for misunderstandings.

•In professional aviation communication, focusing on clear, objective, and respectful language is crucial for safety and effective collaboration.

Alternatives:

•To express skepticism about someone's claims, use phrases like "requires further evidence" or "needs more justification."

•To describe someone who talks excessively, use terms like "loquacious" or "verbose."

•To highlight someone's bragging, consider "exaggerated claims" or "boastful statements."

"Get your feet wet" in the context of aviation has two primary interpretations:

1. Literal Meaning:

•This meaning, while rarely used directly, refers to piloting an aircraft over water for the first time. This was originally used by naval aviators when transitioning from land-based operations to carrier landings. Today, it can apply to any pilot experiencing their first water crossing or seaplane operation.

2. Figurative Meaning:

•This is the more common usage, signifying gaining initial experience in any aspect of aviation. It suggests:

•Taking initial steps towards a flying career, like starting flight lessons.

•Participating in introductory aviation activities like attending airshows or museums.

•Trying out new skills or roles within the aviation industry, like learning aircraft maintenance or air traffic control.

Origin:

•The literal meaning likely stems from the actual sensation of flying over water and potentially encountering spray or rougher conditions compared to land.

•The figurative meaning might have evolved from this or simply represent "taking the plunge" into the world of aviation.

Modern Usage:

•Both the literal and figurative meanings are less common today due to:

•Increased availability of flight simulators and training aids.

•Focus on safety procedures and gradual skill development in pilot training.

•Diverse entry points into the aviation industry beyond traditional pilot roles.

Important Notes:

•While not as prevalent, "get your feet wet" can still be used playfully or metaphorically to encourage someone to explore aviation.

•Be mindful of the context and audience when using this phrase, as it might appear outdated or insensitive in some situations.

In aviation, "get off to a flying start" isn't really considered slang, but rather a well-known idiom with a specific meaning:

Original Meaning:

•General: Refers to starting something very well, smoothly, and successfully, like a racehorse out of the gate.

Aviation Context:

•Figurative Use: Applies to:
•Pilots successfully executing a smooth and efficient takeoff and initial climb.
•Airlines launching new routes or services with high demand and positive feedback.
•Aircraft projects experiencing rapid development and successful initial tests.

Modern Usage:

•Widely used within aviation and beyond to describe positive and successful beginnings.

Origin:

•The exact origin is unclear, but likely stems from the general meaning of starting something quickly and positively, combined with the imagery of an aircraft taking off smoothly.

Examples:

•"The new pilot got off to a flying start, impressing instructors with her quick learning and natural talent."
•"The airline's new customer loyalty program got off to a flying start, exceeding expectations with sign-ups."
•"The innovative drone design project got off to a flying start, attracting significant funding and industry interest."

Important Notes:

•"Get off to a flying start" is widely understood and conveys a positive sentiment.
•It's suitable for both formal and informal aviation contexts.

In the context of aviation, "grease it on" doesn't have a well-defined or widely used meaning but here's what I can share:

Possible Interpretations:

•Informal or Figurative: It could be a playful or informal way to describe a smooth and skillful landing. However, this usage isn't common in professional aviation communication due to its ambiguity and potential for misinterpretation.

•Misinterpretation: It might be confused with "grease monkey," which is a slang term for someone who works on the mechanical aspects of vehicles, including aircraft. However, this wouldn't apply directly to the act of landing.

Recommendations:

•Clarity and Precision: In professional aviation settings, it's crucial to use clear and precise language for safety and effective communication. Instead of "grease it on," pilots would use specific instructions and terminology related to landings.

•Alternatives: Phrases like "smooth touchdown," "nice landing," or "firm but gentle rollout" are more appropriate and unambiguous.

Additional Notes:

•Aviation has a rich history of slang and idioms, but these expressions should be used cautiously and only in appropriate contexts to avoid confusion or potential safety risks.

•Always prioritize clear and respectful communication when discussing aviation matters.

In aviation, "go down with flying colours" doesn't hold the same meaning as it does in general language. Here's why:

General Meaning:

•This idiom typically refers to failing at something while putting forth great effort and remaining determined, often used in military contexts where ships wouldn't surrender before sinking.

Aviation Context:

•Rarely used: This specific idiom isn't common in aviation due to its negative connotation of failure, which can be sensitive and inappropriate given the safety-critical nature of the industry.

•Potential Misinterpretation: Mentioning "going down" in aviation can trigger concern or alarm, even if meant metaphorically.

•Alternatives: More suitable phrases to describe overcoming challenges or demonstrating dedication could be "faced obstacles head-on," "maintained professionalism in difficult situations," or "exhibited exemplary composure under pressure."

Important Notes:

•Sensitivity: It's crucial to be mindful of the audience and context when using language in aviation. Jokes or metaphors involving crashes or failures can be offensive or disrespectful to those who have faced loss or trauma in the industry.

•Clarity: Favoring clear and unambiguous communication is key to ensuring safety and effective teamwork.

While "Have a nice flight" certainly has good intentions, it isn't the most common or ideal phrase used in professional aviation communication. Here's why:

Reasons to Avoid:

•Potential Overuse: It's a very general phrase used frequently outside of aviation, which can feel less personal or sincere in a professional setting.

•Focus on Safety: In aviation, the primary concern is always safety. "Have a safe flight" explicitly emphasizes this priority, avoiding the potential for misinterpretation.

•Professionalism: Opting for more specific and professional language demonstrates attention to detail and respect for the importance of the flight.

Alternatives:

•Formal:

•"Wishing you a safe and uneventful flight."

•"Have a pleasant and enjoyable journey."

•"See you at your destination."

•Informal (among colleagues):

•"Smooth skies ahead!"

•"Tailwinds and blue skies!"

•"See you on the other side!"

In aviation, "heads up" holds various meanings depending on the context and tone of voice. Here's a breakdown:

General Meaning:

•Informal alert: A casual way to warn someone about something they might not be aware of or need to pay attention to.

•Cautionary: Used to emphasize potential dangers or obstacles ahead.

•Informative: Sharing an update or important information quickly and concisely.

Aviation Context:

•Formal use: Less frequent in formal communication due to potential ambiguity. Precise terminology is preferred for safety reasons.

•Informal use: More common among pilots and air traffic controllers in casual interactions.

•Examples:

•Pilot to copilot: "Heads up, turbulence ahead."

•Air traffic controller to pilot: "Heads up, traffic at your 12 o'clock, 2 miles."

•Ground crew to pilot: "Heads up, maintenance work in progress around runway 18."

Important Notes:

•Clarity is crucial: Ensure the intended meaning is clear and avoids confusion, especially regarding safety-related matters.

•Formal settings: Use clear and specific terms instead of "heads up" for clarity and professionalism.

•Consider alternatives: Phrases like "be aware," "important information," or "potential hazard" might be more appropriate depending on the situation.

"Hit the ground running" is a widely used idiom that can apply to aviation in a few different ways:

Literal Meaning:

•For military aircraft, "hitting the ground running" could literally describe a touchdown with a hard impact, although this isn't ideal and pilots strive for smooth landings.

Figurative Meanings:

•More commonly, "hitting the ground running" figuratively describes:

•Starting a new role or project in aviation quickly and efficiently, without delay. This could apply to new pilots starting their careers, airlines launching new routes, or aircraft manufacturers initiating new projects.

•Being fully prepared and ready to take action upon arrival or activation. This could describe emergency response teams at airports, rescue helicopter crews, or military pilots responding to a situation.

Considerations:

•While "hitting the ground running" can convey positive qualities like initiative and efficiency, it's important to remember that safety is paramount in aviation. Rushing or compromising procedures should never be encouraged.

•In formal communication, more specific language might be preferred to avoid ambiguity. For example, instead of saying "hit the ground running," you could say "begin operations immediately" or "transition swiftly to active status."

Alternatives:

•For starting new roles or projects: "begin immediately," "commence operations promptly," "transition quickly to full functionality."

•For being prepared and ready: "on high alert," "fully operational upon arrival," "prepared for immediate action."

"Holding pattern" is a common and well-defined term in aviation with a specific meaning. It doesn't fall into the category of slang or idiom, but rather technical terminology. Here's a breakdown:

Definition:

•A holding pattern is a predetermined, racetrack-shaped flight path used by an aircraft to maintain position while awaiting further clearance. This is commonly used when:

•Air traffic is congested and the aircraft needs to wait before landing.

•Weather conditions temporarily prevent landing.

•An emergency necessitates temporary holding of the aircraft.

Key elements of a holding pattern:

•Entry procedure: Specific instructions for joining the pattern from the current position.

•Holding fix: A designated point where the aircraft enters and exits the pattern.

•Legs: Straight flight segments composing the rectangular shape of the pattern.

•Turns: Standard directions and angles for turns (usually 45 degrees or 180 degrees).

•Holding altitude: Specific altitude maintained while in the pattern.

Additional notes:

•Holding patterns are designed to keep aircraft separated and ensure safe operations during delays.

•Pilots follow published procedures and instructions from air traffic control for specific holding patterns.

•The duration of a holding pattern can vary depending on the situation.

Alternatives:

•In informal contexts, phrases like "circling overhead" or "waiting in a loop" might be used loosely, but it's important to be aware of the technical differences.

"Kick the tires and light the fires" is a well-known aviation expression, though its usage and interpretation can vary depending on the context:

Original Meaning:

•This phrase originated in the early days of aviation, when pre-flight checks often involved physically kicking the tires to test their pressure and visually inspecting the engine for proper startup procedures.

Modern Interpretations:

•Formal: Often used in military contexts to order flight crews to prepare for immediate takeoff. This emphasizes immediacy and readiness for action.

•Informal: Commonly used as a motivational phrase to encourage enthusiasm and eagerness to start something new, not necessarily limited to aviation.

•Figurative: Used metaphorically to embrace new challenges, take risks, and jumpstart projects with energy and optimism.

Important Notes:

•While widely recognized, "kick the tires and light the fires" can seem informal or outdated in some professional aviation settings.

•Safety comes first: This phrase shouldn't be taken literally as modern aircraft require far more complex pre-flight procedures.

•Alternatives: In formal contexts, more specific and professional language like "prepare for immediate departure" or "initiate takeoff sequence" is preferred.

In aviation, "Knife Fight in a Phone Booth" isn't a common expression with a specific meaning directly related to flying. However, it can have metaphorical interpretations depending on the context:

Possible Interpretations:

•Urban Warfare Analogy: This phrase, used more broadly in military contexts, describes intense, close-quarters combat in a confined space, potentially representing:

•Dogfighting maneuvers between fighter jets engaging in close combat.

•Difficult landing conditions with limited space and high pressure.

•Complex emergency situations requiring quick, decisive action in confined environments.

•Informal Hyperbole: It could be used informally to exaggerate the challenging or stressful nature of a specific situation, not necessarily limited to aviation.

Important Notes:

•Using "Knife Fight in a Phone Booth" in aviation contexts can be ambiguous and potentially offensive due to its violent connotation.

•Clarity and professionalism are crucial in aviation communication, especially when discussing emergencies or complex maneuvers.

•This phrase doesn't accurately reflect the sophisticated technologies and procedures used in modern aviation.

Alternatives:

•For dogfighting: "Engaging in close-quarters aerial combat," "performing high-G maneuvers."

•For difficult landings: "Challenging approach with limited visibility," "requiring precise control for safe touchdown."

•For emergency situations: "Responding to a critical event," "implementing emergency procedures efficiently."

"Lighter than air" is a widely used term in aviation, although not exactly slang or an idiom. It holds a specific and important meaning:

Literal Meaning:

•Refers to any aircraft or object that can achieve buoyancy and fly due to being lighter than the surrounding air. This includes:

•Hot air balloons: Heated air inside the envelope makes them lighter than air.

•Blimps and airships: Filled with helium, a gas lighter than air, they achieve buoyancy.

•Gliders: Utilize their aerodynamic design to create lift even without an engine.

Figurative Uses:

•Less common, it can be used metaphorically to describe something:

•Free-spirited, carefree, or unburdened by worries.

•Idealistic or imaginative, having unique perspectives.

•Fragile or vulnerable, requiring careful handling.

Important Notes:

•"Lighter than air" has a precise meaning in aviation and shouldn't be confused with "light aircraft" (referring to smaller airplanes compared to airliners).

•While generally understood, using it figuratively in aviation conversations is less common and requires careful consideration of the context to avoid misinterpretation.

Alternatives:

•Formal contexts: "Buoyant aircraft," "aerospace vehicles utilizing lighter-than-air technology."

•Informal contexts: "Free-flying," "imaginative," "delicate."

"Living the dream" is a widely used idiom that carries a variety of connotations depending on the context. Here's a breakdown:

Meaning:

•On the surface, "living the dream" signifies experiencing great satisfaction and fulfillment, having achieved your aspirations and leading an ideal life. It implies happiness, success, and enjoying what you do.

•However, it can also be used sarcastically, to mock someone portraying their life as perfect despite obvious issues or difficulties.

Origin:

•The exact origin is unclear, but it first appeared in the early 20th century, gaining popularity in the 1950s and 60s.

•It's likely linked to the idea of the "American Dream" – achieving social and economic success through hard work and determination.

Interpretation:

•When someone says "living the dream," it's important to consider their tone and context. Are they genuinely expressing contentment, or are they being ironic or humorous?

•Additionally, the "dream" itself is subjective and individual. What constitutes a dream life varies greatly from person to person.

Overall:

•"Living the dream" is a versatile phrase that can carry different meanings depending on the situation.

•It's a good idea to interpret it based on context and personal understanding of the speaker's situation and intent.

"Mayday" is an internationally recognized distress signal, used only in life-threatening emergencies. It signifies that an aircraft or vessel is in grave danger and requires immediate assistance.

History:

•Coined in the early 1920s by Frederick Mockford, a senior radio officer at Croydon Airport in London.

•Derived from the French "m'aider," meaning "help me."

•Chosen for its clarity and ease of pronunciation in various languages.

Usage:

•Repeated three times in a row ("Mayday, mayday, mayday") to ensure it's not mistaken for another transmission.

•Followed by essential information like aircraft identification, nature of the emergency, and location.

•Triggers an immediate response from air traffic control or other emergency services.

Importance:

•Critical tool for saving lives: By alerting authorities quickly, it allows for faster intervention and potential rescue.

•Standardized procedure: Ensures everyone understands the severity of the situation and can react accordingly.

•Used responsibly: Misusing "mayday" for non-emergency situations can delay response to actual emergencies.

"On course" has two main meanings, depending on the context:

1. Making progress towards a goal:

•This is the most common meaning of "on course." It means that things are progressing as planned and you are likely to achieve your goal.

•This could apply to various situations, such as:

•A project: "The project is on course to be completed by the deadline."

•A personal goal: "I'm on course to lose 10 pounds this month."

•A competition: "The team is on course to win the championship."

•In aviation, specifically, "on course" typically indicates that the aircraft is following its intended flight path and is not experiencing any navigational issues.

2. Staying on the chosen path:

•This meaning implies that things are proceeding smoothly and without any major diversions or disruptions.

•This could apply to:

•A conversation: "Let's stay on course and avoid getting sidetracked."

•A meeting: "We need to get back on course and finish the agenda."

•Life in general: "I'm trying to stay on course and avoid negativity."

Additional factors:

•The phrase "on course" can be further modified by adverbs to indicate the degree of progress. For example, "well on course" implies significant progress, while "barely on course" suggests potential challenges.

•Depending on the situation, "on course" might be used optimistically to express confidence in achieving a goal, or neutrally to simply state the current progress.

"Out of thin air" is a commonly used idiom with interesting meanings and applications. Here's a breakdown:

Meaning:

•Sudden and unexpected: This is the core meaning of the phrase. It describes something that appears or happens abruptly and surprisingly, as if it materialized from nowhere.

•Unfounded or unsubstantiated: It can also imply that something is imaginary, fabricated, or lacks a clear basis, suggesting it's just made up or pulled out of nowhere.

•Miraculous or magical: In some contexts, it can carry a sense of wonder, suggesting something improbable or impossible happening unexpectedly.

Examples:

•Suddenly: "He pulled a rabbit out of thin air, leaving the audience speechless."

•Unfounded: "She accused him of making up stories out of thin air."

•Miraculous: "The rescue seemed to come out of thin air, a true stroke of luck."

Origin:

•The exact origin is unclear, but it likely emerged from the idea of air being empty and intangible. Imagining something appearing from such emptiness created the association with unexpected or impossible occurrences.

Interpretation:

•The nuance of the phrase depends on the context. Consider the tone and surrounding information to understand if it refers to suddenness, lack of basis, or a miraculous event.

Application:

•"Out of thin air" is a useful phrase to describe unexpected surprises, unfounded claims, or seemingly impossible occurrences.

•Use it carefully, being mindful of the potential interpretations depending on the context.

In aviation, "pushing the envelope" is indeed a well-established idiom. It refers to operating an aircraft close to or beyond its known performance limits. This can involve exceeding:

•Speed: Flying faster than the recommended or safe airspeed.

•Altitude: Climbing higher than the certified ceiling of the aircraft.

•Maneuverability: Performing tight turns, stalls, or other demanding maneuvers outside of routine operation.

•Load factors: Subjecting the aircraft and occupants to high g-forces.

It's important to understand that pushing the envelope is inherently risky. While test pilots and experimental aircraft might intentionally do this in controlled environments to understand an aircraft's capabilities, it's generally dangerous and discouraged for normal flight operations.

Here are some additional points to consider:

•Degree of risk: Pushing the envelope can range from slightly exceeding limits for a brief moment to venturing far beyond them, resulting in significantly increased risk of accidents or structural failure.

•Context: In certain situations, like avoiding an emergency, pilots might need to make calculated decisions to momentarily push the envelope to ensure safety. However, this needs to be a last resort and done with extreme caution and expertise.

•Professionalism: Responsible pilots prioritize safety and remain within the designated flight envelope. While pushing the envelope might seem exciting or impressive, it's not considered a mark of good piloting in professional circles.

Overall, "pushing the envelope" is a powerful idiom in aviation, conveying the concept of testing boundaries and taking calculated risks.

While "Roger" itself isn't technically an idiom, it is a widely used term in aviation communication with a specific meaning. Here's what you need to know:

Meaning:

In aviation, "roger" simply means "I have received and understood your message." It acknowledges that the message has been heard and comprehended.

History:

•"Roger" originated from the use of the letter "R" in morse code to signify "received." In the early days of aviation radio, pilots simply said "R" instead of spelling out the entire word.

•Later, as voice communication became standard, "roger" was adopted as the spoken equivalent of "R" due to its familiarity and ease of pronunciation.

•In 1957, the phonetic alphabet changed "R" to "Romeo," but "roger" remained ingrained in aviation communication.

Important notes:

•Although widely used, "roger" does not imply agreement or willingness to comply with an instruction.

•Pilots are expected to read back instructions verbatim to ensure clear understanding and avoid miscommunication.

•In modern aviation, "roger" is less common as pilots prioritize precise phraseology to avoid any ambiguity.

Alternatives:

•"Affirmative" - Used to confirm agreement or willingness to comply.

•"Wilco" - Combination of "roger" and "will comply," indicating both understanding and agreement.

•Specific acknowledgements - Used for certain instructions, like "cleared for takeoff" or "squawk 7000."

"Something is in the air" is a common idiom with a few different interpretations depending on the context. Here's a breakdown:

Meaning:

1.General feeling or atmosphere: This is the most common interpretation. It suggests that a particular mood, sentiment, or anticipation is present, even if it isn't explicitly stated or discussed. The feeling could be positive (excitement, celebration), negative (tension, nervousness), or simply a sense of change or something brewing.

2.Unseen but pervasive influence: Here, the idiom implies that something intangible but impactful is affecting people or circumstances. This could be an upcoming event, a brewing conflict, a new idea gaining traction, or even something intangible like a cultural shift.

3.Intuition or premonition: In some cases, "something is in the air" can suggest a gut feeling or intuition that something significant is about to happen, even without concrete evidence. It's akin to sensing a change in the wind before a storm.

Origin:

The exact origin is unclear, but it likely stems from the physical experience of sensing changes in the atmosphere, which can precede weather events or signify broader environmental factors. The metaphorical use evolved from this literal meaning.

Examples:

•"There was a sense of excitement in the air as the concert neared."

•"Tension is in the air between the two companies as merger talks escalate."

•"I just have a feeling something big is in the air, but I can't put my finger on it."

Interpretation:

Understanding the specific meaning of "something is in the air" depends on the context and surrounding information. Consider the tone, setting, and what else is being said to grasp the specific mood or influence being implied.

"To clear the air" is a well-known idiom with a clear and consistent meaning. Here's what you need to know:

Meaning:

•To address and resolve misunderstandings, tensions, or disagreements openly and honestly.

•To remove any emotional negativity or confusion that might be hindering communication or relationships.

•To create a more open and positive atmosphere for conversation and understanding.

Application:

•This idiom can be used in various situations, from personal relationships to professional settings.

•It can involve open conversations, apologies, explanations, or simply acknowledging and discussing the issue at hand.

•The goal is to "clear the air" by addressing the root cause of the problem and moving forward on a more positive note.

Examples:

•"I think we need to clear the air about what happened yesterday."

•"Let's have a conversation to clear the air and avoid any misunderstandings."

•"I apologize for my actions, and I hope we can clear the air and move forward."

"To clear the air" is a straightforward and helpful idiom for expressing the desire to openly address and resolve issues, leading to better communication and understanding. Remember that it doesn't guarantee a specific outcome, but sets the intention for constructive dialogue and progress.

"To have your nose in the air" is a classic idiom with a negative connotation. It means:

Meaning:

•To behave in a haughty, arrogant, or condescending way.

•To think you are superior to others and act in a way that reflects that belief.

•To be disdainful or dismissive of others.

Origin:

The idiom likely comes from the physical image of someone holding their head high with a slight upward tilt, as if looking down on someone else. This posture can be seen as arrogant or snobbish.

Examples:

•"She walked past us with her nose in the air, like she didn't even see us."

•"He always speaks to me with his nose in the air, like I'm beneath him."

•"Don't act like you have your nose in the air, just because you got a promotion."

It's important to note that:

•The interpretation of "having your nose in the air" can depend on the context. In some cases, it might simply mean someone is aloof or uninterested, rather than deliberately arrogant.

•Using this idiom can come across as harsh or judgmental, so it's best to use it with caution.

While "touch and go" isn't necessarily an established idiom in aviation, it does accurately describe a common maneuver performed during flight training and sometimes real-world operations. Here's the breakdown:

Meaning:

In aviation, a "touch and go" is a landing followed immediately by a takeoff without coming to a complete stop on the runway. This typically involves:

1.Landing: The aircraft approaches and touches down on the runway.

2.Brief roll: The aircraft briefly rolls down the runway, usually maintaining low speed.

3.Acceleration and liftoff: Power is added, and the aircraft accelerates and takes off again before reaching the end of the runway.

Purpose:

This maneuver is used for several reasons:

•Training: Pilots practice landings, takeoffs, and transitions between the two in a short timeframe, increasing proficiency and efficiency.

•Expediency: In situations where runway availability is limited and multiple aircraft need to land, touch and go landings can allow more landings to occur than full stops.

•Maintaining currency: Pilots can fulfill currency requirements for specific landing types by performing touch and gos.

Important notes:

•Touch and go landings require specific authorization from air traffic control and adherence to established procedures.

•They aren't always appropriate, depending on weather conditions, traffic volume, and other factors.

Similar terms:

•Stop and go: Landing, coming to a complete stop, and then taking off again.

•Low pass: Flying low over the runway without touching down.

"Up in the air" is a versatile phrase with several common meanings depending on the context. Here's a breakdown:

1. Uncertain or undecided: This is the most common meaning of "up in the air." It signifies that something is not yet settled, determined, or planned. The outcome is unknown, and it's impossible to say for sure what will happen.

•Examples: "Our vacation plans are still up in the air." "The future of the company is up in the air after the merger."

2. Indefinite or unclear: This meaning suggests that something is vague, ambiguous, or lacking concrete details. There's a lack of clarity, and it's difficult to understand the full picture.

•Examples: "The rumors about the new product are all up in the air." "His instructions were very up in the air, leaving me confused."

3. Not grounded or established: This meaning implies that something is unstable, temporary, or lacking a solid foundation. It's subject to change or disruption.

•Examples: "His career was up in the air after the scandal." "The peace treaty seems up in the air due to recent tensions."

4. Invigorating or exciting: In rarer cases, "up in the air" can have a positive connotation, particularly when referring to activities or experiences. It suggests a sense of adventurousness, thrill, or anticipation.

•Examples: "The roller coaster ride had me up in the air with excitement." "The prospect of starting a new business has me up in the air."

Understanding the specific meaning:

To understand the exact meaning of "up in the air" in a given situation, consider the context, tone, and surrounding information. Look for clues in the conversation or text that point towards uncertainty, indefiniteness, instability, or even excitement.

In the context of aviation, "wingman" is indeed an established and well-known idiom, carrying significant meaning and responsibility. Here's what you need to know:

Meaning:
•A pilot flying alongside and in support of another aircraft, typically in a formation.
•The "wingman" positions themselves slightly behind and off to the side of the lead aircraft, maintaining visual contact and providing protection, backup, and assistance.
•This role requires exceptional teamwork, situational awareness, and piloting skills to ensure the safety and success of the mission.

Responsibilities:
•Maintaining formation: Staying in the designated position relative to the lead aircraft.
•Monitoring potential threats: Watching for other aircraft, weather hazards, or any danger to the lead.
•Providing support: Relaying information, acting as a backup in case of emergencies, and helping with navigation.
•Protecting the lead: Taking defensive actions if necessary to shield the lead aircraft from threats.

Origin:
The term originated from military aviation, where wingmen played a crucial role in protecting bombers and other vulnerable aircraft during combat missions. The concept later adopted a broader meaning within all formations, signifying teamwork and mutual support.

Modern usage:
While the core concept of supporting and protecting the lead aircraft remains, the application of "wingman" in modern aviation has evolved:
•Civilian formations: Used in recreational flying and aerobatic performances for safety and coordination.
•Search and rescue operations: Aircraft fly in formation to maximize coverage and communication.
•Air racing: Wingmen provide tactical advice and support to their racing partners.
•

Beyond aviation:
The concept of "wingman" has expanded beyond its literal meaning, symbolizing loyalty, collaboration, and unwavering support in other contexts. It signifies having someone you can rely on, who has your back in challenging situations.

"Wing it" is a widely used informal phrase, not specifically an aviation idiom, but with a clear meaning across various contexts. Here's what you need to know:

Meaning:
•To do something without much preparation or planning.
•To improvise, make it up as you go, relying on your wit and resourcefulness.
•To act spontaneously and deal with situations as they arise.

Examples:
•"I didn't have time to prepare, so I had to wing it during the presentation."
•"We forgot the ingredients for dinner, so we just winged it and made something delicious."
•"Let's just wing it and see what happens tonight."

Origin:
•The exact origin is unclear, but it likely emerged from the theater world, where actors might have to replace someone suddenly and "wing it" by learning their lines on the fly.
•Over time, it expanded to various situations where improvisation and quick thinking are needed.

Connotations:
•"Winging it" can have positive or negative connotations depending on the context.
•Positively, it can portray resourcefulness, adaptability, and a willingness to embrace the unknown.
•Negatively, it can imply a lack of preparation, carelessness, or recklessness.

Similar expressions:
•Improvise
•Freestyling
•Making it up as you go
•Thinking on your feet
•Off the cuff

Overall:
"Wing it" is a versatile phrase that effectively conveys improvisation and spontaneous action. Use it carefully, understanding its context and potential interpretations to be clear and avoid unintended meanings.

While "with flying colors" isn't strictly an aviation idiom, it is widely used within the aviation community in the same way it is in general language. Here's a breakdown:

Meaning:

•To succeed exceptionally well, to demonstrate excellence.

•To achieve something difficult or challenging with impressive results and beyond expectations.

Examples in aviation:

•"The pilot landed the aircraft with flying colors despite the strong crosswinds."

•"The student pilot passed their check ride with flying colors, demonstrating their mastery of the skills."

•"The new aircraft design completed its test flight with flying colors, exceeding all performance expectations."

Origin:

•The phrase originates from the maritime tradition, where ships returning from successful voyages would proudly fly their flags. Conversely, unsuccessful ships wouldn't display their flags. This symbolism of visible achievement evolved into the phrase "with flying colors" to represent exceptional success in various contexts.

Application in aviation:

•Pilots and other aviation professionals strive to perform "with flying colors" in various aspects of their work, including:

•Safe and efficient flight operations: Landing smoothly, navigating challenging conditions, or responding effectively to emergencies.

•Training and proficiency: Successfully completing checkrides, demonstrating mastery of new skills, or excelling in theoretical knowledge.

•Collaboration and teamwork: Working seamlessly with colleagues to achieve common goals and ensure flight safety.

Overall:

While not a unique idiom to aviation, "with flying colors" effectively conveys the spirit of excellence and exceptional achievement within the industry. It highlights the dedication, skill, and professionalism required in various aspects of aviation operations.